Miracles of
Jesus

Illustrated by Toni Goffe
Retold by LaVonne Neff

Tyndale House Publishers, Inc.
WHEATON · ILLINOIS

EG

Published in the United States by
Tyndale House Publishers, Inc.
Wheaton, Illinois
Published in Great Britain by
Hunt & Thorpe

ISBN 0-8423-3970-1
Printed in Singapore

01 00 99 98 97 96 95 94
9 8 7 6 5 4 3 2 1

Contents

Jesus Says No to Satan

Matthew 4:1-11; Mark 1:12-13; Luke 4:1-13

Jesus had spent forty days in the wilderness. He had not eaten any food, and he was hungry.

One day Satan came to him. "If you are God's Son," said Satan, "turn stones into bread."

Jesus answered, "Scripture says that God's Word is more important than bread."

Satan then took Jesus to a high place. "If you are God's Son," he said, "jump off, and let God save you."

Jesus answered, "Scripture says, 'Don't put God to a foolish test.'"

Then Satan showed Jesus all the kingdoms of the world. "These kingdoms are mine," he said. "Worship me, and I will give them to you."

Jesus answered, "Get out of here, Satan! Scripture says, 'Worship only God.'"

Jesus knew he was God's Son. He knew that the whole world belongs to God. He would not do any miracles for Satan. He would do them only for God.

Jesus Turns Water into Wine

John 2:1-12

There was a wedding at Cana in Galilee. Mary, the mother of Jesus, was invited, and so were Jesus and his disciples.

In the middle of the feast, the wine ran out. Mary said to Jesus, "They have no wine." Then she said to the servants, "Do whatever Jesus tells you."

Nearby were six huge stone jars. Jesus said to the servants, "Fill the jars with water."

The servants filled them to the brim.

"Now dip some out," said Jesus, "and take it to the man in charge of the feast."

When the man tasted what the servants brought him, he was amazed. He went to the bridegroom and said, "Most people serve the good wine first, but you have kept the best wine for last!"

This was Jesus' first miracle. When his disciples saw it, they believed in him.

Jesus Calms the Storm

Matthew 8:23-27; Mark 4:35-41; Luke 8:22-25

It was evening, and Jesus was tired. "Let's cross the Sea of Galilee and rest," he said to his disciples.

The men set sail. Jesus lay down in the back of the boat and fell asleep.

Suddenly a fierce wind arose. Huge waves crashed against the little boat. Water poured over the sides, and the boat began to sink.

Jesus was still fast asleep. The disciples called out to him, "Don't you care that we are drowning?"

Jesus got up. He faced the howling wind and roaring waves. He raised his arm and said, "Peace! Be still!"

Instantly the wind stopped. The waves flattened out. The night was calm and still.

Jesus turned to his disciples and said, "Why were you afraid? Where was your faith?"

The disciples were amazed. They said to each other, "Who is this man? Even the wind and the sea obey him!"

Jesus Casts Out Demons

Matthew 8:28-34; Mark 5:1-20; Luke 8:26-39

There was a wild man living in a graveyard near the Sea of Galilee. Night and day he ran naked across the mountains, screaming. People said he had a demon.

One day the man saw Jesus. He ran to him and knelt down. Jesus knew that many demons lived in the man. He ordered them all to leave.

Nearby was a herd of two thousand pigs. "Send us into those pigs," the demons said.

Jesus agreed. Suddenly the pigs began to scream. Then they stampeded down the mountainside into the sea.

Many people went out to see what had happened. They found the wild man sitting next to Jesus. The man was wearing clothes. He was talking quietly.

Frightened, the people begged Jesus to leave. The wild man asked Jesus, "May I go with you?"

"No," said Jesus. "Stay here and tell everyone what God has done for you."

Jesus Heals a Paralyzed Boy
Matthew 9:1-8; Mark 2:1-12; Luke 5:17-26

In Capernaum lived a boy who could not walk. His friends put him on a stretcher and took him to Jesus.

People packed the house where Jesus was preaching. They blocked the door and the windows. The men could not get inside. So they climbed onto the roof, removed some tiles, and lowered their friend through the opening.

Jesus saw that the boy had faith. "Son," he said, "your sins are forgiven."

Some people whispered to each other, "Only God can forgive sins!"

"Which is easier to say," Jesus asked them, "'Your sins are forgiven,' or 'Get up and walk'? I will show you that I can forgive sins."

Jesus turned to the boy. "Get up, take your stretcher, and go home," he said. The boy got up and ran through the crowd.

The people were amazed. They said to each other, "We have never seen anything like this!"

Jesus Raises Jairus's Daughter

Matthew 9:18-19, 23-26; Mark 5:21-24, 35-43; Luke 8:40-42, 49-56

One day a ruler named Jairus came to Jesus and knelt down. He said, "My only child is dying. If you will lay your hand on her, she will live."

Jesus started to follow Jairus, but soon a messenger ran up. "Sir, your daughter has died," he said. "There's no need for Jesus to come now."

Jesus kept on walking. "Do not fear; only believe," he said.

When they arrived at Jairus's home, they could hear people crying. "Why weep?" Jesus asked. "The girl is not dead. She is sleeping." The people laughed at him.

Jesus went with the girl's parents into her room. He reached out and took her hand. "Little girl, get up," he said.

Immediately the girl sat up and got out of bed!

"Give her something to eat," Jesus said.

Soon everyone for miles around was talking about the raising of Jairus's daughter.

Jesus Feeds Five Thousand

Matthew 14:13-21; Mark 6:30-44; Luke 9:10-17; John 6:1-14

Wherever Jesus went, huge crowds followed. They wanted to hear him teach. They wanted to see him heal. Sometimes they forgot all about eating.

Late one afternoon, the disciples said to Jesus, "It's time to send the people away to buy food."

Jesus replied, "Why don't you give them something to eat?"

The disciples did not have any food. Andrew said, "There is a boy here with five barley loaves and two fish, but what are they among so many?"

"Bring them here to me," Jesus said.

Jesus took the boy's food. He gave thanks for it, broke it, and gave it to the disciples.

The disciples started passing out the bread and fish. The more they gave away, the more they had! There was more than enough bread and fish for the whole crowd.

The people said to one another, "Jesus really is the prophet we have been expecting."

Jesus Walks on Water

Matthew 14:22-33; Mark 6:45-52; John 6:15-21

The disciples finished gathering up the leftovers from the meal of loaves and fishes. Jesus told them to take their boat and cross the Sea of Galilee. He stayed behind to say good-bye to the crowd. When he was finally all alone, he went to a quiet place to pray.

That night the wind was strong and the waves were high. The disciples rowed for many hours. They were tired.

Suddenly they saw a man walking on top of the sea. He was coming straight toward them. "It is a ghost!" they cried out.

Then they heard a familiar voice. "Don't be afraid," Jesus said. "It is I."

Jesus climbed into the boat with the disciples. Immediately the wind died down, and the boat arrived safely at its destination.

The disciples were amazed. "Truly you are the Son of God!" they said.

Jesus Heals Ten Lepers

Luke 17:11-19

In Jesus' day, people with leprosy could not live with their families. Wherever they went, they had to shout, "Unclean! Unclean!" so people could stay away from them. Most lepers never got well.

One day ten lepers met Jesus. "Jesus, Master, have mercy on us," they called out.

Jesus said to the ten lepers, "Go and show the priest that you have been healed."

The lepers looked at their bodies. Marks of leprosy were still there. But they believed Jesus, and they set off to find the priest. While they walked, their leprosy disappeared!

One of the lepers immediately turned around and ran back to Jesus. He knelt at Jesus' feet. "Thank you, Jesus," he said.

Jesus helped the grateful man stand up. "I healed ten men," he said. "Where are the other nine? Are you the only one who is praising God for being healed?"

Jesus Promises More Miracles
John 14:1-14

Jesus and his disciples were eating their last meal together. Jesus would soon be going home to his Father in heaven. The disciples were worried. They did not know what would happen to them.

Jesus saw that his friends were lonely and confused. "Don't be afraid," he said. "My Father has been doing wonderful things through me. When I leave, he will do even greater miracles through you. He will do whatever you ask in my name."

Soon the disciples understood Jesus' words.

In Jesus' name, they healed the sick, raised the dead, and cast out demons.

In Jesus' name, they told the whole world that the Father loves us, that Jesus died for us, and that the Spirit gives us life.

From their day to ours, millions of people have followed Jesus. And that is the greatest miracle of all.